BOSTON

FROM THE AIR

BOSTON

FROM THE AIR

Elizabeth McNulty

Thunder Bay
P·R·E·S·S

Published in the United States
Thunder Bay Press
An imprint of the Advantage Publishers Group
5880 Oberlin Drive, San Diego, CA 92121-4794
www.advantagebooksonline.com

Produced by PRC Publishing Ltd
Kiln House, 210 New Kings Road
London SW6 4NZ

All notations of errors or omissions should be addressed to Thunder Bay Press,
editorial department, at the above address. All other correspondence (author inquiries,
permissions and rights) concerning the content of this book should be addressed to
PRC Publishing Ltd, Kiln House, 210 New Kings Road, London SW6 4NZ.

ISBN 1-57145-275-3

Library of Congress Cataloging-in-Publication Data available upon request.

Printed and bound in China

1 2 3 4 5 00 01 02 03

For Lisa, Gautam, and Kasturi, great friends with whom I first explored this great city.

INTRODUCTION

With her infamously "crook'd and narrow" streets, grown haphazardly, organically, and above all, densely over 350-plus years of history, Boston is the driver's curse and the walker's dream. Around each corner lurks another architectural treasure just waiting for the pedestrian to reach the right viewpoint. However, cities consist not just of buildings, but of streets and neighborhoods, not to mention natural (and in Boston's case, unnatural) geography, and it is the rare city where all this can be glimpsed by the person on foot. What better way to view a city founded on the sea, reclaimed from the river, and possessed of notoriously labyrinthine roadways, than from the air?

Boston from the Air provides, most literally, an overview of one of America's best-loved cities, and in so doing, offers the joy of rediscovering famous landmarks, historic districts, and contemporary architecture from a new vantage point. Aerial photography highlights the contrast between the 18th century Boston of Beacon Hill, with its picturesque cobblestone streets and classic Boston bow fronts, and the 19th century Boston of Back Bay, with its Parisian boulevards and Victorian mansions. It also contrasts Boston's low-rise, five-story historical roofline and the 20th century's "high spine" of skyscrapers stretching the length of the city. Photography from above shows green space and monuments in their context of cityscape and even makes it possible to get to know tall and distant towers up-close and personal. Two things immediately become apparent from the air: that the city is geographically intimate with the waterfront, and that the city is bursting at the seams with sites and structures of historical import.

Boston was founded by Puritans in 1630 on a narrow spit of land known as the Shawmut Peninsula. Even after the ambitious landfilling program of the 19th century when Boston tripled its original size with the addition of Back Bay, and even after annexing surrounding suburbs and whole cities (Charlestown, Dorchester, South Boston, etc.), Boston still constitutes only about 50 square miles of land. However, the city is also divided up by ocean, river, and canal; neighborhoods less than a few blocks away from one another retain their distinctive characters. On foot, the neighborhoods contain such a wealth of interest that it seems to take forever to move across town. Above the city, viewing this crabbed landmass from the air, we instantly see the proximity: almost every frame shot downtown contains either the Park Street Church or the Custom House Tower, and the Hancock Tower can be used to orient just about everything else. Close quarters and ubiquitous waterfronts are part of Boston's unique

identity as America's earliest city; they are part of what makes the city so "livable," so "walkable," and the reason why every last block has twice its share of American history.

From the oldest colonial Blackstone Block to Paul Revere's North End to the Boston Brahminland of Beacon Hill, Boston packs in history by the century. The buff could write pages inspired by a single aerial photo of Faneuil Hall. And what a photo! Owing to Boston's close quarters, the same frame would also feature Quincy Market, Dock Square, the Custom House Tower, the Blackstone Block, the Haymarket, etc., etc. (see page 27). Boston is famous for her neighborhoods, and no wonder, given the immense variety enfolded into small areas. In the North End, from the air we glimpse a scene frozen in history. When the Central Artery cut the North End off from downtown, it simultaneously preserved it as the best example of 18th century Boston, an area true to the city's original height limits, where church steeples still dominate the sky. Government Center, just a few feet away, provides a dramatic contrast, where city planners ripped out whole streets, replacing them with a new kind of monumental cityscape, perhaps best appreciated from above. We see Boston's Financial District, where contemporary skyscrapers crowd the waterfront and compete with original Boston Granite–style buildings. Back Bay's broad vistas and sprawling Charles River playground belie its length of just eight blocks. It is amazing to see how the South End and Roxbury sit less than ten blocks from the Pru. It is also amazing to see Logan Airport in the background of almost every waterfront scene; it is less than two miles from downtown, after all. From the Harbor Islands to the Emerald Necklace of parks throughout the city, to next-door neighbor Cambridge, *Boston from the Air* presents a wealth of spectacular views of an historic, but often hard-to-see city.

Note—Thriving cities don't sit still, and Boston is no exception. Part of what we see from the air is a continuation of Boston's constant evolution. Since colonial days, the city has constantly redesigned itself, leveling hills and building land where once there was waterfront. Today, Boston is home to the largest, most complex and technologically challenging highway project in American history, the "Big Dig," as it's called, underway since 1991, is a plan to enlarge and move the Central Artery underground. When the project is completed in 2004, the downtown will have 27 new acres of open space, mostly parkland, and the North End will be symbolically reunited with the city. In the meantime, photographs throughout the downtown area show cranes, workers, and torn-up streets.

Founded in 1634, just four years after the establishment of the city, Boston Common is the oldest public park in America. These 50-some acres have seen a variety of uses, from troop marshaling and cattle grazing (finally outlawed in 1830), to the dispensing of public justice (including hangings). Three of the five borders of the common are seen here (*left to right*): Beacon, Park, and Tremont streets. The Frog Pond at lower left has not yet been filled for summer.

Seen here in context, with Beacon Hill filling the foreground, the Common seems to form a sort of boundary between Old Boston, with her red-brick row houses punctuated by the spires and domes of church and state, and downtown's New Boston, with, as one commentator put it, "her soaring towers of commerce," Boston's unique 20th century skyline. Crisscrossed by well-worn paths, the Common is also Boston's most human space, and the considerable heart of the city.

Designed by famed early-Boston architect Charles Bulfinch, the State House, with its signature gilded dome and classical red-brick construction, dominates the Beacon Hill skyline. It is hard to imagine the building as it appeared in 1797 with a whitewashed wood-shingled dome and by the 1820s, marble-painted walls. It wasn't until 1861 that the dome was gilded (in 23 karat gold sheeting), and it has only been darkened once, during threat of air raid in World War II. The dome is topped with a gilded pinecone, a symbol of the vast forests of then northern Massachusetts (today, Maine). The photo at right gives an idea of Bulfinch's original. The rear extension was added in the 1890s, and the marble wings in 1917. Statues of famed orator Daniel Webster and educator Horace Mann flank the entrance.

Park Street runs between the State House and the church. Originally the city outskirts, Park Street was once home to a poorhouse, a jail, and an insane asylum. With the construction of Bulfinch's State House in 1797, the street became a fashionable district. Bulfinch also designed a string of houses lining the street, which came to be known as Bulfinch Row. Of them, only the Armory-Ticknor, here under scaffolding, remains.

PARK STREET

Park Street Church was designed by English architect Peter Banner and built in 1810 on the grounds of an old granary, thus the name of the Granary Burying Ground beside it where repose such Revolutionary heroes as Samuel Adams, John Hancock, and Paul Revere. The corner of Park and Tremont is known as "Brimstone Corner," as much for the church preachers as for the use of the church crypt to store gunpowder during the War of 1812. At lower left is the Park Street Station, the first depot in the first subway in America, established 1897. The bright red line on the sidewalk, emerging from the Common, then continued in brick down Tremont Street, maps out the Freedom Trail. Boston's most popular tourist attraction, the Freedom Trail is a walking tour past the city's most historic sites.

Left: "The sunny street that holds the sifted few," as Oliver Wendell Holmes famously characterized it, Beacon Street runs across the photo at the foot of Beacon Hill's south slope. The street affords gorgeous views across the common and features some of the best examples of that most classic Boston architectural style: the Boston bow front (see the Somerset Club at right for a somewhat exaggerated example). The South Slope, once pastureland owned by painter John Singleton Copley, became the locus of Boston Brahmin power and prestige in the 19th century.

MOUNT VERNON STREET

Quiet, tree-lined Mount Vernon Street was called "the only respectable street in America" by American novelist Henry James, one of the district's many literary notables. Others who lived in the vicinity included Louisa May Alcott, Robert Frost, even Mark Twain and Charles Dickens for a time. In the foreground stands the Charles Street Meeting House, designed in 1804 by Asher Benjamin. About midway back at left, the treetops mark Louisburg Square, the only park on Beacon Hill.

Left: Pinckney (*lower right corner*), called "Cinderella Street" by one author, along with Myrtle Street (*right*) formed the unofficial dividing line between sunny, dignified South Slope and the windy, Bohemian North Slope of Beacon Hill. Revere Street is at center. The North Slope became the hub of several 19th century immigrant communities, including the Irish and Jewish. Just around the corner from Revere off Joy Street stands the African American Meeting House. Government Center is in the background.

The Asher Benjamin–designed Charles Street Meeting House, with its graceful Federal lines and white cupola, played an important role in the antislavery movement in Boston as the site of several historic abolitionist speeches. Today, the meeting house contains shops and offices. At left stands the Gothic-revival Church of the Advent (1888), the Episcopal house of worship for many of Boston's most famous socialites. Legend has it that flamboyant patron Isabella Stuart Gardner once had to scrub the church steps for Lenten penance.

Left: Fanciful Longfellow Bridge, connecting Beacon Hill with eastern Cambridge across the Charles, is sometimes known as the "pepperpot" bridge because of its castellated mini-towers which are reminiscent of salt-and-pepper shakers. It was designed in 1907 by Edmund March Wheelwright, who modeled it on a bridge in St. Petersburg, Russia. Beacon Hill fills the foreground. At the edge of the river, sailboats are at anchor in the protected area near the Community Boathouse.

At the foot of Beacon Hill's North Slope, Cambridge Street forms a sharp divide between the historical Beacon Hill neighborhood (*right*) and the urban-renewal West End (*left*) and Government Center (*straight ahead*), where most buildings date from the mid-20th century. Only a few older buildings were preserved during the wholesale razing of the West End neighborhood in the late 1950s.

View up Stanford at Cambridge Street. In the left foreground stands Old West Church, one of the few historic buildings left in the West End. Completed in 1806, it was designed by Asher Benjamin, who designed the Charles Street Meeting House a few years prior. The architecture of both buildings is in the elegant, flat-faced, Federal style of Charles Bulfinch, Benjamin's mentor. Today, after a stint as a library branch, Old West is restored and in use as a Methodist Church.

Back Bay and parts of Beacon Hill were subject to the ebb and flow of the tide until the construction of the first Charles River Dam in 1910. A new, three-lock dam was constructed in 1978, with one of the most powerful pumping stations in the country; the old dam was also preserved, but left standing open. In 1951, the Museum of Science moved into these unusual digs perched atop the dam to become a Boston landmark. The Hayden Planetarium is the dome at left.

Along with Old West and the Otis House, one of the few old buildings left standing in the West End after urban renewal in the late 1950s is the Suffolk County (Charles Street) Jail. Now standing beside the renowned Massachusetts Eye and Ear Infirmary, the Quincy granite building was designed in 1851 by Gridley Bryant with the assistance of noted prison reformer Rev. Louis Dwight and was considered innovative for its use of natural light.

WEST END

With the rear addition of Beacon Hill's State House in the immediate foreground, this view looks due north over the West End. This area was razed in the late 1950s with two notable exceptions: Old West Church (built 1806, designed by Asher Benjamin), at center, and to its left, the Harrison Gray Otis House (built 1796, designed by Charles Bulfinch, now home to the Society for the Preservation of New England Antiquities). At right, the FleetCenter.

Seen from the air, this area is a nest of highways, train tracks, and river roads. North Station hubs all the commuter trains from the North Shore and in summer time is thronged with crowds awaiting the beach train. At center is Interstate 93, the Fitzgerald Expressway. At left is the Leverett Circle Connector Bridge, part of the Big Dig project opened October 1999. At right, the historic Charlestown Bridge. The FleetCenter, which replaced its beloved predecessor, the Boston Garden, in 1995, is home to Celtics basketball and Bruins hockey.

The cobblestone island at center marks roughly where stood the original Scollay Building, which gave rise to the moniker Scollay Square, an area infamous for its seedy nightlife, tattoo parlors, and burlesque palaces. In the early 1960s, the city completely razed the area to create Government Center. The gilded Steaming Kettle, hanging from the Sear Block at left, has been a local landmark since 1875. At top, the verdigris dome of the Old City Hall and the squat tower of King's Chapel.

I. M. Pei and Partners crafted the master plan for Government Center, carving out from the historic (but rundown) Scollay Square area, a 56-acre site for city, state, and federal offices. McKinnell & Wood, who won a national competition for this project in 1968, designed the new City Hall at center. To the right, the 26-story John F. Kennedy Federal Office building rises from the broad red-brick plaza. One Center Plaza (*center*) gracefully echoes the historic Sears Crescent (to the upper left of City Hall).

Pemberton Square, at the eastern foot of the hill, was once one of only two squares on Beacon Hill (the other, Louisburg Square, still survives). The construction of the grandiose French Second Empire-style court house in 1896 marked the beginning of this formerly residential neighborhood's transition. Today, the Suffolk County Court House faces a brick plaza lined by One Beacon (*background*) and One Center Plaza (*left*).

Left: Nestled between the hulking behemoth that is Government Center and the Central Artery (soon to disappear thanks to the Big Dig), stand the Faneuil Hall and Quincy markets (*left*) and the historic Blackstone Block (*right*). It seems almost impossible to believe that the area directly in front of Faneuil Hall was once known as Dock Square because it abutted the water and contained the city's municipal dock. In the 19th century Bostonians built land out of what was once Town Cove.

A gift to the city from Huguenot merchant Peter Faneuil in 1742, Faneuil Hall earned the nickname "Cradle of Liberty" during the Revolutionary War, when it was the site of anti-British orations by patriots like Sam Adams and James Otis. By 1806, the market crowds were so great that Charles Bulfinch was enlisted to enlarge the Hall to its present size. Today, the Hall houses a variety of merchants and restaurants and is one of Boston's most popular tourist destinations.

The 535-foot long Greek Revival building with the copper dome was named not for the Quincy granite used in its construction, but for then-mayor Josiah Quincy who proposed this extension of the Faneuil Hall Market. Designed by Alexander Parris in 1826, Quincy Market was for over 150 years the premier meat and produce wholesalers' venue in the city. In the 1970s, the entire marketplace was renovated with cafes, bars, and boutiques.

Look closely at the base of this building and you will see a Greek Revival temple designed by Ammi Young in 1847. For over 50 years, the original Custom House sat on the water's edge, then in 1915, after landfill moved it inland, the Federal government decided to slap a 495-foot tower on it. Peabody and Stearns designed the graceful extension. It was Boston's first skyscraper and New England's tallest building for decades.

The best preserved section of colonial Boston, the Blackstone Block was named for the original settler Rev. William Blaxton (so he spelled it). The names of these tiny, cobblestone streets, Marsh Lane, Creek Square, etc. reflect the pre-landfill proximity of the waterfront. The corner building with the three dormer windows (*center right*) is the Union Oyster House, established 1715, the city's oldest restaurant. At lower right, is the New England Holocaust Memorial, dedicated in 1995.

On Friday and Saturday, Blackstone Street, along the edge of the Blackstone Block, is transformed into an open-air market of pushcart vendors, selling fruits, vegetables, fish, and seafood. The colorful market, here partially under sunshade, is always crowded with people (as well as crushed boxes and some squashed produce underfoot). Since many of the merchants are North Enders, this event is sometimes called the Italian Market.

Cut off from downtown since the construction of the Central Artery (left) in the 1950s, the North End has maintained its historic character perhaps better than any other Boston neighborhood. It is Boston's original neighborhood where Puritans settled in the 17th century, and where waves of immigrants made their homes in the 1800s. It has been Boston's historic Italian neighborhood for the last 70 years, as witnessed by the many annual *feste*, or Italian saint's day celebrations.

Built circa 1677, the oldest house extant today in Boston is decidedly Tudor in style, with its low-profile two stories, overhanging jetty, and leaded casements. Paul Revere and his family lived here (1770–1800), and the house is now a museum. The three-story next-door neighbor is the Pierce-Hichborn House (1711), the oldest surviving brick residence in Boston. There is an authentic colonial herb garden behind the houses. At far right, the Mariners' House, dedicated to the service of seamen since the 1870s.

Two of the North End's most famous churches, Old North (*foreground*) and St. Stephen's (Bulfinch's sole surviving church) are linked by a stretch of park called the Prado. It is also known as the Paul Revere Mall on account of the bronze equestrian statue of Revere on his "midnight ride," just barely visible on the Hanover Street end between the treelines.

The oldest church building in Boston, Christ Church, or Old North as it is popularly known, was designed by William Price in the style of Christopher Wren and completed in 1723. It was from Old North's nearly 200-foot steeple that church sexton Robert Newman hung the lanterns "one if by land, two if by sea" to warn colonists of the British advance.

The widest, straightest street in the otherwise "crook'd and narrow" North
End, Hanover Street is the district's commercial heart, lined with cafes,
restaurants, and shops. Two of Boston's department-store tycoons started
business here: Eben Jordan of the Jordan Marsh Company, and Rowland Macy
of Macy's. One hundred years later, in 1996, the latter purchased the former.

On Hanover Street at Prince in the North End. The first Italian church erected
in New England, St. Leonard's was designed in 1891 by William Holmes. Next-
door is St. Leonard's Church Peace Garden, planted at the close of the
Vietnam War, and maintained by two Franciscan friars. It contains two shrubs
from Pope John Paul II's mass on Boston Common in 1979.

With its well-preserved historic streets and buildings, the North End has fewer green spaces than newer Boston neighborhoods, a fact that makes this playground even more greatly appreciated. The area was also home to a bizarre disaster: in 1919, a 50 foot cast-iron storage tank near here burst, pouring out a 2.3 million gallon tidal wave of molasses, and leaving 21 people dead. Cleanup of the sticky syrup was nearly impossible, and North Enders claim the aroma still lingers on warm days.

Boston's fortunes were founded on the sea, and the multitude of wharves bears out the importance of both the shipping and fishing industries in Boston's history. The Bay State Lobster Company is the East Coast's largest seafood operation and has been in business for over 70 years, supplying Bostonians with everything from fresh fish and lobsters to clam chowder to lobster pie. In the background, churches still dominate the skyline. The tree-lined area at right is one of Boston's historic cemeteries, Copp's Hill Burying Ground.

Charlestown burned during the Revolution, and the citizens struggled to rebuild. The city's recovery was aided in 1800 with the founding of the United States Charlestown Navy Yard, a source of good jobs for over 150 years. The Yard was decommissioned in 1974, but is now a National Historic Park, with most of its 19th century structures intact: see the red-brick Commandant's House set back on the green lawn and Dry Dock 1 at center.

The Charlestown Naval Yard's most famous resident, the U.S.S. *Constitution*, is the oldest commissioned naval vessel in the world. Launched in 1797, she is nicknamed "Old Ironsides" not for any metal plating, but for the tough oaken hull that was seemingly impervious to bullets in the War of 1812. In a normal year, the ship makes one tour, the "turnaround" every Fourth of July.

Rising above Monument Square, with its carefully preserved 1840s town houses, the Bunker Hill Monument took 18 years to complete before being dedicated in 1843. Around midnight on June 16, 1775, colonists began building a fortification on what they took to be Bunker Hill; by daylight, they realized they were atop Breed's Hill. The battle was fought there and the misnomer remains. Although the British took the hill, they suffered devastating losses. This 220-foot tall obelisk of Quincy granite commemorates this battle, when the colonial militia was reportedly ordered not to fire "until you see the whites of their eyes." For those willing and able to climb the 294 steps, the monument provides sweeping views of Boston.

Charlestown predates Boston. Founded in 1629 by Puritans, some of whom later moved across the river, Charlestown was a thriving port town when the British razed it during the Revolutionary War. The citizens rebuilt, and Charlestown became a genteel seaside town of ship captains' homes. It was annexed to Boston in 1874. The graceful arch of Warren Street (*right*), echoed by Main in the middle (*far right*), trace old paths to the long-gone waterfront; just as in Boston, landfill and wharf construction constantly redesigned the shore. The large granite church (*above*) is St. Mary's, built 1892 on the exact

site of the first settler's plot. The pale yellow, three-story square Warren Tavern (*left*, at foot of Warren Street). It was the first building erected after the British burning of Charlestown and is named in honor of General Joseph Warren, who died in the battle. At far right, the green leafy area is Town Hill and Harvard Mall, dedicated to Charlestown resident John Harvard, who donated his fortune and library toward the establishment of the university.

Charlestown has a wealth of beautifully preserved historic buildings, from many periods and styles. A small stretch of downtown Main Street captures the wide variety. At left, the Federalist, red-brick row houses of early Boston. At center, the mansard-roofed Savings Bank Building, a gorgeous Victorian Gothic from 1876. Center right, a home in the utilitarian style the citizens hastily constructed after the British razed the city (see the Warren Tavern). At right, a variation on the classic, high-Boston "bowfront."

One of the oldest burial grounds in the country, Phipps Street would originally have faced lovely
seaside views on three sides, but landfill in the 1800s changed the terrain. "Burying Hill," as it was
first called, holds over a thousand pre-1800 and 300 pre-1700 burials. It narrowly escaped the
British destruction in 1775, and only then because it was not affiliated with any church. Some of
Boston's best examples of early American tombstones can be seen here.

When the Mystic River Bridge opened in 1950, at two and a quarter miles, it was the longest cantilevered-truss bridge in the country. Renamed in 1967 in honor of Boston politico Maurice J. Tobin, the bridge stretches from Charlestown over the Mystic River into Chelsea. The bridge's blue-green girders have become a landmark, beloved by some, disliked by others who believe the construction destroyed historic Chelsea.

The view beyond the Tobin Bridge out toward Boston Harbor on a crystal-clear
November day. At left, Chelsea and then further out, Winthrop. Slightly to the right
and straight ahead is Logan Airport, and beyond it Deer Island. Off in the far right
distance, the Harbor Islands. In the far distance, the country's oldest lighthouse, the
Boston Light, can just barely be seen, gleaming white on Little Brewster Island.

The Puritans first settled in Boston because it had plentiful fresh water and a large, deep, natural harbor. Passing between Dorchester and Logan Airport, and heading straight for the downtown area, the waterway is known as the inner harbor. These natural attributes, formerly so important for Boston's shipping-based economy, are now enjoyed mostly by pleasure cruisers and personal sailboats.

Two miles east of downtown, Logan Airport sits on an East Boston peninsula. While other cities have witnessed their airports drawing business away from the city center, Logan's handy location (it is literally a seven minute journey by water taxi to reach the financial district) has helped keep business in the harbor port. The airport handles more than 50 domestic and international airlines in its five terminals, and has just celebrated the 75th anniversary of its first passenger flight.

The inner harbor extends all the way back beyond the North End (*left,* with Old North End steeple) to Charlestown (*straight ahead*, Bunker Hill Monument) with a natural, relatively deep channel. The many wharves jutting out from these two old communities suggest the great historic importance of maritime trade in Boston.

The downtown wharves, vestiges of Boston's maritime industries, were all converted to commercial purposes in the 1970s and 1980s, an effort that reinvigorated the then-rundown waterfront. The first project was the boxy, concrete New England Aquarium on Central Wharf, which was completed in 1969. Soon after, in 1971, the I. M. Pei–designed, luxury-condo, twin Harbor Towers went up on India Wharf.

Unlike the India and Central Wharf developments, which seem constructed in spite of their harborside locale, the 1987 Rowes Wharf development of shops, offices, and condos is widely admired for taking its inspiration from the past. The graceful archway echoes an arch in the original structure; the use of traditional red brick and simple geometric shapes evokes the old colonial warehouses.

The Waterfront & Faneuil Hall Market BOSTON

...y's oldest wharf, Long Wharf was constructed in 1710. At the time it was almost ...mile long, but by the 20th century landfill and road construction had significantly ...hed it. Redevelopment in the 1980s saw construction of the hulking brick Boston ...t, but thankfully preserved the 1763 brick Gardner Building (where John Hancock ...d an office) and the 1847 granite Custom House Block.

Boston's wharves underwent major commercial redevelopment in the 1970s and 1980s, erasing much of the evidence of their gritty industrial past. The Fort Point Channel, on the other hand, harks back to what the entire waterfront must have looked like at the turn of the 20th century. This narrow band of water is all that separates Boston from South Boston, which was but a distant neck of land before the massive landfilling of the Shawmut Peninsula in the 1800s. The piers at left are: the Fish Pier, location of the New England Fish Exchange, and the beflagged Commonwealth Pier, an enormous convention-type trade center.

In the 1870s, the Boston Wharf Company cut the Fort Point Channel and built warehouses in South Boston to store a variety of goods, from sugar and fruits to lumber and coal. The area lost prosperity in the early 20th century, with the decline of the fishing, shipping, and manufacturing industries, but is being revitalized today with an influx of artists and urban pioneers. Where Summer Street crosses the channel stands the gracefully curving Melcher Street warehouse.

Griffin's Wharf succumbed to landfill long ago, but somewhere near the spot seen here, in December 1773, angry colonists, dressed as Mohawk Indians, tossed overboard 340 chests of expensive British tea to protest a newly imposed tax. At anchor in the Fort Point channel along the Congress Street bridge rests the *Beaver II*, a Danish brig resembling one of the three original ships boarded by colonists, it is anchored beside the Tea Party Museum.

With One Financial Place to the north, South Station tracks and the Postal Annex to the east, and the big nest of highways to the south, the Leather and Garment District is limited to just seven blocks. The Great Fire of 1872 hit this neighborhood hard, and all of these buildings date to within the three decades after the fire. Today, this area is touted as the "SoHo" of Boston with artist studios, serious galleries, and a high-style restaurant scene.

Since the 1950s, the Central Artery has cut off the city from the waterfront, and North End from downtown. Today, the largest, most complex and technologically challenging highway project in American history is underway to enlarge and bury the Central Artery underground. Begun in 1991, and slated for completion in 2004, the "Big Dig," as the project is known, is currently at the peak period of construction and is completing roughly $3 million worth of work each day. At any one time, about 4,000 construction workers and 150 cranes are in use on the project. When complete, the project will open up 27 acres of parkland downtown, where the existing elevated highway now stands, and will reduce carbon monoxide pollution by up to 12 percent by alleviating gridlock.

At Summer Street and Atlantic Avenue. Completed in 1899, and designed by Shepley, Rutan, & Coolidge, South Station was the largest train depot in the world and also the busiest, peaking in 1913 with 38 million passengers a year—more than New York's Grand Central Station. It now houses Amtrak, commuter trains, and the red line, in addition to shops and offices. The headquarters of the "Big Dig" are located here, and out front, Big Dig construction is in full swing.

SUMMER STREET

View west up Summer Street. South Station is at lower left, with One Financial Place (1983) looming behind. Across from the giant stands 125 Summer Street (1990), perhaps the best example of the "historic skirt" style of preservation, where older buildings are preserved at street level as part of the new development. The aluminum-clad Federal Reserve Bank of Boston (1977) stands at right. Beacon Park Street Church steeple and one wing of Bulfinch's State House appear with the rest of Beacon Hill at upper right.

DOWNTOWN CROSSING

Washington Street between Summer and Bromfield. The stretch of Washington where Summer turns into Winter has been a shopping mecca since the early part of the 20th century. By the 1970s, the area was named Downtown Crossing; the streets were bricked and made a pedestrian mall. The eight-story Beaux-Arts building at bottom center is Filene's, one of the original Boston department stores. Designed by Daniel Burnham in 1912, it features white-glazed terra cotta with verdigris-colored ornamentation. Filene's still occupies the site. The copper-covered dome in the background is Old City Hall.

DOWNTOWN CROSSING
Bromfield crossing Washington. At the corner, the Beaux Arts "skyscraper," the Jewelers Building (1898), which still houses nearly 100 jewelry dealers.

Washington is one of the oldest streets in Boston, forming the original thoroughfare from State House to the neck of the Shawmut Peninsula. As such, it has always been a commercial and cultural center. This section of Washington Street south of Downtown Crossing is part of Boston's historic theater district. From left: the Paramount, Boston's best Art Deco theater, built in 1932 exclusively for films; the Savoy, originally B. F. Keith Memorial Theater by Thomas Lamb, 1928. The original "vaudeville" house with its flamboyant white-glazed terra-cotta facade in the Spanish Baroque style, this theater was most recently known as the Opera House, while the Opera Company of Boston occupied it. The Modern, Boston's first movie theater, was set up in a preexisting Victorian Gothic warehouse (1876). Boston's great theater architect, Clarence Blackall, handled the conversion and interior redesign in 1913. All three of these gems are awaiting restoration.

Known as Piano Row in the 19th century, this stretch of Boylston between Tremont and Charles housed a concentration of piano/organ manufacturers. When "talkies" superceded silent film and live drama, the demand for high-ticket organs plummeted, and so did the businesses. At far left stand two buildings by Clarence Blackall: the Gothic-influenced Little (1916), and the Colonial (1900, containing the Colonial Theatre). Blackall designed at least 12 Boston theaters, including the Wilbur and the Metropolitan (now the Wang Center for the Performing Arts).

The area between the Central Artery (*center* of photo) and Washington Street in the distance, and between Kneeland Street (*left*) and Essex is Boston's tiny, four-block-wide Chinatown. Early Chinese immigrants to Boston arrived with the increase in the China trade shortly after the Revolutionary War, but it was not until 1875 that a permanent community was established. Today, the neighborhood is shared with southeast Asian immigrants and is credited with decreasing crime in the nearby "Combat Zone," Boston's red-light district on south Washington.

Washington Street at Milk. The second oldest church in Boston (after Old North), Old South was built in 1729 as both a house of worship and a town hall, and later became famous as the launch point for the Boston Tea Party. In retaliation, the British commandeered the structure during their occupation of the city, stripping the interior, and housing their cavalry within. Old South narrowly escaped the Fire of 1872, and now contains a permanent history exhibit.

Near right: View up narrow Tremont Street. King's Chapel and Burying Ground peeks from between the newly restored 73 Tremont Building (1896) at left and the Tremont Temple (Clarence Blackall, 1896) at right. Built on a corner of Boston's oldest burying ground, King's Chapel was founded in 1686. Funds ran out before architect Peter Harrison's spire could be built so this squat Georgian chapel in Quincy granite was considered complete in 1754. After the Revolutionary War, the chapel became the first Unitarian church in America.

Right: Looking down School Street from Washington. Built during the Civil War and designed by Back Bay planner Arthur Gilman, Old City Hall is a fine example of French Second Empire architecture, with its copper-plated mansard roof in the style of the Louvre. Today, Old City Hall is hailed as an early example of "adaptive re-use." It was converted to house offices and restaurants when Government Center was built. King's Chapel and Burying Ground stand at the corner.

OLD STATE HOUSE

Looking west down State Street with Big Dig in the foreground, the Old State House does resemble, in the words of one commentator, "a dollhouse" among giants. From left to right: 75 State Street (with the gold ornament), the Custom House Tower against the mirrored Exchange Place, the black Boston Company Building, the pink 60 State Street Building, and Faneuil Hall and Quincy Market against the backdrop of Government Center. Built in 1713, the Old State House was the center of social and political life for the colonists. It was from this balcony that the Declaration of Independence was first read to Bostonians on July 18, 1776. The cobblestone circle on the traffic island visible in the photo at right marks the location of the Boston Massacre of 1770, when British soldiers fired on a colonial mob.

CUSTOM HOUSE TOWER

Although Boston had a 125-foot building height limit at the turn of the 20th century, the federally owned Custom House property (at that time a four-sided Greek temple), was not subject to local ordinances. During an economic decline of the waterfront area, the federal government funded the addition of a 16-story tower to the temple structure, and thus was built Boston's first skyscraper. Initially scorned as a preposterous yoking of styles, the Custom House Tower has become the signature silhouette on Boston's skyline. At left, the 75 State Street Building (Skidmore, Owings & Merrill, 1988), with its verdigris-tinted windows and gold-leaf decoration, pays clear homage to the tower. At right the early 20th-century tower creates a picturesque contrast with its 18th-century neighbors. The 22-foot-wide clock is lit from within at night.

At one time the Custom House was so close to the water that ships could bump the front steps. After years of landfill, the narrow and crooked blocks near the tower reflect older shorelines. At lower left, the Central Artery cuts past the Flour & Grain Exchange and beside it, the eight remaining brick Central Wharf Buildings, designed by Charles Bulfinch.

Broad Street was one of several ambitious 19th century redevelopment schemes. Laid out circa 1805 according to Charles Bulfinch's plans, it was lined with Federal-style warehouses, of which only a few remain. On State Street at Broad (*top*) stands the Richards Building (1867), with its distinctive pair of two-story oriel windows at either end. It is one of the only cast-iron façade buildings in Boston.

FLOUR & GRAIN EXCHANGE

Milk Street at India. The Flour & Grain Exchange is a whimsical triangular building, constructed in 1893 by Shepley, Rutan, & Coolidge. However, their mentor Henry Hobson Richardson's influence is strongly visible in the Romanesque arches and heavy granite exterior. A conical roof and a circuit of pointed dormers tops the rounded corner, suggesting a crown. Originally built for the Chamber of Commerce, today the Flour & Grain Exchange houses architects' offices.

LIBERTY SQUARE
From over the Insurance Exchange Building down Crab
Alley (Water Street is to the right, both names a reminder
of the waterfront's former proximity). Liberty "Square" is
actually a triangle where six of the city's old, narrow 17th
and 18th century streets intersect. At the end of the 18th
century, a 60-foot liberty pole was set up here to com-
memorate the Stamp Act riots. Today, a sculpture commemorates the Hungarian Revolution of 1956. The rounded
building is the Appleton (1926).

FINANCIAL DISTRICT TEXTURES

In 1872, some passersby noticed flames in a wholesale drygoods house. Some 24 hours later, the heart of downtown Boston stood in ruins, 65 acres in all, 800 buildings. The Great Boston Fire razed the entire business district, from the waterfront (including several ships) all the way to Washington Avenue. In its wake, the fire left a clean slate for building, and the financial district remains the main focus of Boston's 20th century architecture.

A view due west from the waterfront, the luxury condos in I. M. Pei's Harbor Towers (1971) on India Wharf loom in the foreground with the State Street Bank Building (1966), and behind it, the Shawmut Bank Building (1975). At left, there is a corner of the Philip Johnson's International Place (1985). The two John Hancock Towers, the stepped pyramid top (1947) and the glassy landmark (1975) are at right, their size making Back Bay seem quite close.

FINANCIAL DISTRICT TEXTURES

The white Keystone Building at 99 High Street (1970), with its repetitive bows, has been called "the beehive." An early Art Deco skyscraper, the United Shoe Machinery Building (1930), features various setbacks and a truncated pyramid of gold tile. The crenellated roofline of the State Street Trust (1929), another Art Deco jewel, is just visible at the left. The Bank of Boston (1971), sometimes called the "Pregnant Building" for its cantilevered midsection bulge, stands tall at center.

More examples of 20th century architecture, including two of Boston's most disliked. Crammed into a tiny 2.6 acre space, formerly Fort Hill, International Place (Philip Johnson, 1985) has been called "a highly visible representative of the worst of the overdevelopment of the 1980s." Nonetheless, these highly geometric shapes with their repetitive patterns make a striking presence on the waterfront. At left, the gold-trimmed building that has been called the "Tammy Faye Baker of architecture," 75 State Street.

Sometimes called "the Washboard Building," the Federal Reserve Bank's unique structure helps reduce tall-building downdraft and the aluminum skin reduces solar heat gain. One Financial Place (1983) at right is the only building in Boston clad with a precast-concrete rain-screen system developed in Canada that minimizes leakage. The base of the building is granite to better relate to the opposing South Station at street level (hidden behind the Fed here).

In the 1970s, this triangle of land, called in the quaint Boston style a "square," contained an ugly city parking garage. By the 1980s, a private initiative was underway to restore the square, and seven layers of parking are now buried underground. At lower left, the top of the "Art Moderne" New England Telephone Building (1947). At center, resembling a throne, Boston's best-known Art Deco, the McCormack Post Office (1931). The gold-eagle-topped column marks the Angell Memorial Fountain, a watering spot for horses built 1912.

A southwest view that presents a wonderful assortment of complementary geometric designs from many architectural eras. In the foreground, the Flour & Grain Exchange (1893) with its rounded corners. Across the street, the 20 and 21 Custom House Street Buildings. The first to be developed in response to the Boston Redevelopment Authority's 1986 guidelines, they are built of granite like their neighbors, and modest in size and style. At center, the round-cornered Appleton Building (1926) on Liberty Square, and finally the Art Deco McCormack Post Office (1931).

Many of downtown Boston's historic landmarks can be seen in this view. The 20th century buildings, excluding Government Center, seen here are (left to right): One Beacon (rose granite), Post Office (throne), Boston Company Building (black), 28 State Street (brownish bilevel towers), Exchange Place (iridescent glass), 60 State (pink ribbed granite behind Exchange), and 75 State Street. Locate the gold-topped cupola of the Old State House at center; directly across from it, with the Romanesque arches, stands Boston's first granite skyscraper, the Ames Building (1889).

Downtown seen from over the common. The column on Flagstaff Hill is a monument to the Union soldiers and sailors of the Civil War. The cement-lined Frog Pond is at left, here not yet filled for the summer. Tremont Street, lined with high-rise condo and apartment buildings, edges this eastern end of the common. Logan Airport is visible in the distance.

The Public Garden was once a soggy, salt-marsh, flooded by the Charles River, and hemmed by rope footbridges off which the locals clammed and fished when the tides allowed. In 1859, Bostonians voted the garden forever public and set about landscaping it as one of the country's earliest botanical gardens. The four-acre lagoon has been home to the famous swan boats since 1877. One of many statues in the garden, Thomas Ball's equestrian statue of George Washington (1869) faces Commonwealth Avenue.

Until the launch of an ambitious landfill project in 1857, Back Bay was also a marsh. Over 30 years, the city leveled off its hills, as well as carting in rock and dirt from elsewhere, in order to create land. By the 1880s, Boston's landmass was triple its original size. However, the Charles was still a polluted tidal estuary until 1910 when the Charles River Dam was built, transforming this stretch beyond the Longfellow Bridge into a beautiful recreational area.

A striking departure from 18th century Boston's crooked and narrow streets, Back Bay became an emblem of 19th century Victorian planning. Inspired by Napoleon's Parisian boulevard system (designed by Baron Haussmann), architect Arthur Gilman designed an orderly grid layout for the streets, complete with a broad central mall and half-width alleys to allow for service and deliveries. The area quickly became the most desirable address in the city. Despite the French design inspiration, the cross streets are named for British peerages: Arlington, Berkeley, Clarendon, etc.

At 240 feet wide, Comm Ave is just slightly wider than the street on which it was modeled: Paris' Champs-Elysées. The central mall is 100 feet across and punctuated by statuary throughout. The Ave is famous for its display of blooming magnolias in spring, but is lovely year-round: when densely shaded in the summer heat, when the leaves turn fiery in autumn, and in winter when the bare trees allow spectacular views of what has been called the finest collection of Victorian architecture in America.

Copley Square was originally a gravelly plot where two rail lines interrupted Back Bay's meticulous grid. The first Museum of Fine Arts was located here, and thus the area became known as "Art Square," and later, in 1883, "Copley" after the great colonial painter, John Singleton Copley. Bordering the square are Trinity Church, the John Hancock tower, the Copley Plaza Hotel, and the Boston Public Library. In 1969, the diagonal of Huntington Street was removed, creating an actual square of the formerly triangular lawn.

Designed by Henry Hobson Richardson, and completed in 1877, this massive, granite masterpiece of French-Romanesque style (now known as Richardson Romanesque) weighs 90 million pounds, and sits on 4,500 wooden pilings to support it in Back Bay's gravel landfill. Next-door to Trinity Church, where once stood the original Museum of Fine Arts, stands the venerable, red-awninged Copley Plaza Hotel, host to gala social events, presidents, and royalty since its opening in 1912.

Boston claims the country's oldest public library, founded 1848. The BPL had outgrown its original location on Boylston overlooking the common, when McKim, Mead, & White were commissioned to design a new building on Copley Square, marking the shift of Boston's cultural center to Back Bay. Completed in 1895, the Italian Renaissance palazzo-style library turned a new corner in American architecture. Today, the BPL is the second largest public library in the country, serving over two million people yearly.

Completed in 1875, this Northern Italian Gothic church became the new home of the Old South Meeting House congregation. Cummings & Sears designed the building with multicolored stonework, tall campanile, and copper-topped Venetian lantern. In the 1930s, the tower was found to be leaning, due to a combination of the soft fill of Back Bay and the construction of Copley subway station. The tower was replaced with a smaller one, a subtle change thanks to reuse of the original stone.

Left: When Back Bay was developed, the Charles River was a smelly mudflat during low tide, and thus houses along Beacon Street were built with their "backs" to the river. Finally, in 1910, the Charles River Dam was built, transforming this stretch of waterfront into a freshwater city lagoon and recreational area, called the Esplanade. The protective green island is the Charles River Embankment. Storrow Drive (1951) unfortunately cut the park off from easy pedestrian access, but there are several footbridges.

Right: The Esplanade refers to the entire grassy riverbank past the Longfellow Bridge. Where the sailboats are at anchor stands the Union Boat Club, America's oldest rowing club, founded in 1851. The concrete dome structure, built in late Art Deco style in 1940, is the Hatch Memorial Shell where the Boston Symphony Orchestra plays their famed summer Pops program. In the background, Back Bay's most famous skyscrapers, the Hancock Towers.

Back Bay, after landfilling, immediately became the most fashionable residential neighborhood; however some locations were considered more desirable than others. If Comm Ave held the nouveau riche, Newbury Street was said to hold the new "poor." As if there were such a thing in Back Bay! Today, Newbury Street is tied with New York's Fifth Avenue for the highest retail rents in the U.S. (Beverly Hills and Palm Beach rank first and second, respectively). The street is lined with upscale boutiques, galleries, and cafes.

During and after the Great Depression, many Back Bay families could no longer afford to maintain their single-family homes, and subdivided or converted the mansions into apartments. In the late 1960s, developers moved in to create luxury condos out of these historic residences. Already skyscrapers were clustering around the bustling, commercial district of Back Bay, around the irregularly shaped blocks south of Boylston Street, creating an interesting backdrop for the 19th century red-brick homes.

Some of Back Bay's famous skyscrapers look even better up close. At left, the original John Hancock Tower, constructed 1947, now called the 200 Berkeley Street Building. The stepped pyramid is topped with a weather beacon. At right, I.M. Pei's Hancock Tower, completed 1976. This narrow slice of a building, with its smoothly mirrored surface, is widely admired for its beautiful reflections.

The 52-story Prudential Tower, or "Pru" (early 1960s), many-times nominated "least attractive building in Boston."

Philip Johnson's postmodern 500 Boylston Building (1988) has been compared in shape to a 1930s Philco radio. Architects grouse that while it improves the Boylston streetscape with its arched entrance, it has ruined the view of Trinity Church. Substantial public protests attempted to block its construction.

At 62 stories, the Hancock Tower is not only Boston's, but New England's tallest. Designed by I.M. Pei and completed in 1976, the tower got off to a rough beginning for such a famous building. For starters, all the necessary supports sunk into squishy Back Bay soil damaged the historic landmark next-door—Trinity Church—resulting in a protracted lawsuit. Next, inadequate glass was used to sheathe the building, and wind torque caused panels to rain down on the square below. The entire covering was replaced. Then, a final inspection revealed that the building was dangerously unbalanced; extra steel supports were added and a moving weight installed on the 58th floor to counter wind stress. Despite all this, the Hancock is widely admired for the way it fits elegantly into a cramped location, and above all the way it reflects Trinity Church, Copley Square, and even just the golden glow of a late November afternoon.

View down Berkeley Street toward the South End. The original Hancock Building (Cram & Ferguson, 1947) is now known as the 200 Berkeley Building, but the weather beacon still predicts the weather. Before it, the controversial 222 Berkeley Building (by Robert Stern, 1991). The striking Gothic Revival spire of the Church of the Covenant (designed by R.M. Upjohn, built in 1867) marks the corner at Newbury Street. The white-glazed terra cotta, Beaux Arts building at left is the Berkeley Building (Codman & Despredelle, 1905).

Right: View north toward Harvard Bridge. Mass Ave constitutes the western edge of Back Bay, and one of the main north-south thoroughfares. At lower right, a corner of the Berklee Performance Center, affiliated with Boston's famed Berklee School of Music. At Newbury Street there is a striking example of creative renovation: a turn-of-the-century warehouse reworked by Frank O. Gehry in 1989. On the far side of Comm Ave stands the largest mansion in all of Back Bay, built in 1882 for railroad magnate Oliver Ames.

Founded as a colony of religious dissenters, Boston is home to a variety of interesting and historic churches. Back Bay has an abundance, but the most impressive would have to be the world headquarters of the Christian Science Church. Mary Baker Eddy's "prayer in stone," constitutes the simple Romanesque-style square tower and nave in rough granite, built in 1894. By 1906, the massive expansion, including the Byzantine dome, permitted seating for 3,000 members. On the edge of "civility" on south Mass Ave, the Church seemed overwhelmed by commercial neighbors until 1973, when I.M. Pei & Associates devised a 22-acre campus, populated with administrative building. The 28-story Church Administrative Building makes a

nice contrast to the low-slung Colonnade Building, and both form attractive backdrops to the 700-foot-long reflecting pool. The extreme geometrical formalism of landscaping and brickwork have nevertheless created an inviting and well-used human space.

Copper-roofed Symphony Hall (*left*, 1900) on Massachusetts Avenue was the dream of Brahmin philanthropist Henry Lee Higginson, who founded the Boston Symphony Orchestra in 1881. He commissioned McKim, Mead, & White (architects of the BPL) to design this Italianate hall. Considered the "Stradivarius" of concert halls, it was the first built according to newly developed principles of acoustic engineering. The Horticultural Hall (*right*, 1901) across Mass Ave is considered the best example of English Baroque style in Boston; it houses the Horticulture Society's library.

From over the Fens, a view down Huntington Street on a gorgeous clear November day. Symphony and Horticultural Halls face the street beside the Christian Science mother church. Boylston Street's "high spine" of skyscrapers leads to downtown. Northeastern University's campus juts into the foreground. The South End is at right. In the distance, Logan Airport and Deer Island.

In the 18th century, the South End was a desolate marsh except for a narrow, natural causeway along Washington Street called "the Neck," which provided the only approach by land to Boston. Developers filled in the South End 20 years before work began on Back Bay in the 1850s, but once Back Bay was underway, the South End fell out of prominence. For over 100 years, the South End's row houses and Victorian bowfronts have been home to a patchwork of

different immigrants groups, thus becoming Boston's most diverse area. The steeples seen here are All Saints' Lutheran (1899, *foreground*) and Union United Methodist (Estey, 1872). Between the South End and Back Bay

commercial district runs a narrow swathe of greenery, the Southwest Corridor. Cleared to make way for a highway project in the 1970s, community protests were successful in having the strip declared parkland.

Olmsted's transformation of the Fens became the first jewel in his grand scheme for an "Emerald Necklace" of parks across Boston. Today, the Boston Park System is the largest continuous green space throughout an urban American center. From the common and Public Garden (*above*), down the Commonwealth Avenue Mall and including the Esplanade along the Charles River (*right*), out to the Back Bay Fens (*far right*, top) and beyond, the Emerald Necklace incorporates public art, architecture, landscaping, as well as many cultural institutions. The Harvard-run Arnold Arboretum is a living museum for trees, and Franklin Park contains the city zoo. The green spaces serve the community in many ways, including "victory gardens" (*far right*, bottom) where urban dwellers can raise vegetables.

After the landfilling of Back Bay, the Back Bay Fens were a stinking swamp where sewage and run-off drained into the Charles River—not to mention a health hazard. Frederick Law Olmsted, the creator of New York's Central Park, was hired in 1878 to clean up the mess. He installed tidal gates and incorporated a reservoir into the park, with the surrounding land made of newly dredged mud from the basin. The area was transformed into a fashionable center.

Charlesgate, where Stony Brook runs into the Charles, was the original Emerald Necklace connection between the Commonwealth Avenue Mall and the Fens. It has been all but obliterated, however, by the insertion of Highway One and various access roads in the mid-20th century. A friend of park system designer Frederick Law Olmsted, architect Henry Hobson Richardson designed the Romanesque bridge (1880) at lower right, where Boylston Street crosses Stony Brook.

Boston's original MFA was a small group of work donated by Brahmin philanthropists and displayed in the Boston Athenaeum. By 1876, the collection warranted a Ruskinian Gothic palace on newly developed Copley Square, and by 1909, the museum, again in need of space, moved to Fenway. In this large plot beside the Fens, the MFA found a permanent home. The original Classical Revival structure (Guy Lowell, 1909) has been enlarged twice, most recently by the addition of I.M. Pei's west wing at left.

Founded in 1898 to hold evening classes for YMCA members seeking to better themselves, Northeastern University now occupies 60 acres in Boston's "cultural district," between the MFA and Symphony Hall. In designing a campus in 1934 and following, architects Shepley, Bulfinch, Richardson, & Abbott sought to differentiate their image from the classic Anglo-American buildings of Harvard et al. The bulk of the buildings are vaguely Neoclassical, constructed in light gray brick.

Built in 1912, and rebuilt in 1934, Fenway Park's brick and stucco façade is a landmark on Brookline and Yawkey Way. Its peculiar shape is a result of the awkward location, and because adjacent lots were not available during construction. Among the park's other idiosyncrasies is the "Green Monster," the 37 foot wall in left field. Fenway Park is the country's smallest major-league baseball stadium, packing in the majority of fans at the level of

its real grass field. In this era of corporate skyboxes and vast 60,000-seat arenas (Fenway holds 34,000), the park's intimate space is almost a sacred thing for any fan of the good old days of baseball, but especially for Red Sox fans. For precisely these anachronisms, however, the park's days are numbered, and plans for a new stadium are underway.

The intersection where Beacon, Commonwealth, and Brookline intersect was originally known as Sewall's Point; it was the only dry land in the tidal salt marsh that, when landfilled, became Back Bay and Fenway. Today, the square is ground zero for Boston University student life, and the neighborhood claims the lowest median age of any in Boston. On the corner, the BU bookstore occupies the old Peerless Building. It is topped by the local landmark, a 60-square foot, neon Citgo sign. Installed in 1965, the sign was an instant "pop art" hit, and when threatened with demolition in 1982, locals successfully fought to preserve it. This intersection is considered the point at which Boston proper begins where the subway (green line) plunges underground.

With 30,000 students, Boston University is the fourth largest independent college in the United States. Founded in 1839, the university inhabits a large chunk of property along the Charles River west of Kenmore Square, including some historic mostly red-brick townhouses on the Bay State Road. BU became the first college to admit women to all divisions in 1872, and it opened the first American college of music in 1873.

The hybrid-style "BU Bridge," as it is universally known, is the starting point for the world's largest single day regatta, the Head-of-the-Charles. (Note the practicing rowers.) The graffiti on the bridge reflects long-established regional college rivalries. With over sixty colleges and universities, the Boston area is a major center of education and has the highest concentration of students of any metropolitan area in the U.S.

The Charles winding around Harvard. The muddy-green Charles River lazily meanders for 80 miles from Hopkinton to Boston Harbor, a distance of less than 30 miles as the crow flies. Named for England's King Charles I, since earliest colonial days, the river has always been a vital economic force. However, the concentrated industry on the river and the determined landfilling and settlement by inhabitants led to decreased flow and intense

pollution. At low tide in the 19th century, the Charles River became a stinking mudflat (thus Back Bay houses were built facing away from the river to avoid the pollution and accompanying stench). In 1910, the Charles River Dam was built, transforming the basin into a beautiful urban "lake" recreation area. *Above*: the Charles River Esplanade and Back Bay waterfront.

Rowing has been a tradition on the Charles River since colonial days. Although the first boat club was not formed until the 1840s, it was then the first in the nation. At center left, Harvard's picturesque Weld Boathouse, designed by Peabody & Stearns (architects of the Custom House Tower) in 1909.

The elegant John W. Weeks Footbridge, in brick with emblazoned Harvard crests. It is reputedly the best viewpoint to watch the "Head of the Charles" in October. A "four" (four-person boat) passes beneath.

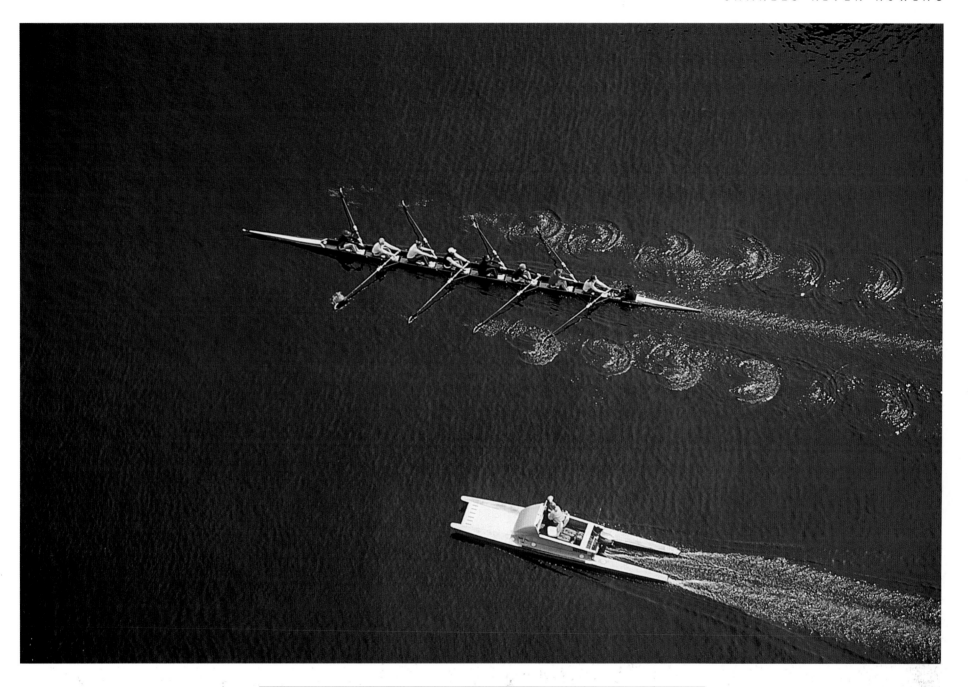

An "eight" practicing under the instruction of their coach. The oldest intercollegiate crew meet in the country is the annual Harvard-Yale competition, first held in 1854, but the biggest single-day regatta is the world-famous "Head of the Charles."

The Charles River is lined on both shores throughout the Boston area with institutions of higher learning. When the Massachusetts Institute of Technology was founded in 1868, it sat on the Boston side of the river. It moved to its current location, on then newly created landfill on the north bank, in 1916. If Harvard is famed for rowing, MIT can claim sport sailing. At the river's edge stands the Walker Wood Sailing Pavilion built in 1935.

MIT's founder, a natural scientist named William Barton Rogers, envisioned a practical institute designed to fulfill the needs of an increasingly industrialized society, and the school has been famous for scientific research ever since. The centerpiece of the campus is the granite, neoclassical

Maclaurin Building (Bosworth, 1916) with its large dome rising over the imposing Ionic portico. Also of architectural note, the tricornered, swooping Kresge Auditorium designed by Eero Saarinen (1955).

Founded in 1643, the first college in the New World, Harvard was originally a divinity school, but relinquished Puritanism in 1865. Today, Harvard is the most famous and, with an estimated endowment of $11.5 billion, wealthiest member of the "Ivy League." With 400 buildings on 380 acres constructed over 350 years, Harvard's architecture runs the gamut, from early 18th century Georgian to 20th century modern. The photo at left is a westward view, with Harvard Yard in the background and the lush summer foliage hiding much of the ground level. At the center, with the white cupola, is Harvard Hall,

designed by Thomas Dawes in 1766. It was the center of the early college. The greenery before it is Harvard Yard. Opposite Harvard Hall is Charles Bulfinch's granite University Hall (1814). The neoclassical, Beaux Arts–inspired building at left is the Widener Library (1913), designed by Julian Abele. The white spire marks Memorial Church, a Georgian imitator actually constructed in 1931.

Memorial (or "Mem") Hall, just north of Harvard Yard is one of only a few examples left in Boston of Ruskinian Gothic style. Harvard graduates William Ware and Henry Van Brunt won a competition to design this cathedral-like structure in 1874 as a memorial to the Harvard students and graduates who had served on the Union side in the Civil War. The "apse" is Sanders Theater, modeled on London's Fortune Theater, and the "nave" is a large hall, originally a dining hall.

Kirkland Street across from Memorial Hall. On the corner sits Adolphus Busch Hall. St. Louis beer magnate Busch, and his wife Lilly, funded this Germanic museum, designed complete with Wagnerian motifs by architect German Bestelmeyer. Although completed in 1917, the museum did not open until 1921 because of anti-German sentiment after World War I. Today, the museum has outgrown the building, and the hall houses Harvard University's Minda de Gunzberg Center for European Studies. The Romanesque hall contains a world-renowned Flentrop organ, used for concerts during the academic year.

Facing the Charles, the expanse of Harvard "houses" or English-style dormitories seems more unified than other parts of the hodge-podge campus, perhaps because many of the buildings were designed by the firm of Shepley, Bulfinch, Richardson, & Abbott in the 1930s. Nevertheless, several of the buildings feature distinctive architectural detail, especially cupolas, which are used as campus landmarks. Together, these buildings constitute Harvard's "Gold Coast."

Left: Lapis-blue cupola sits atop the iterative Georgian-style Lowell House (1930), famed for its bell tower where hangs a set of bells from the Donailov Monastery in Russia.

Center: A gold-leaf trimmed cupola with widow's walk tops Apthorp House (1760), a square Federal-style building part of the Adams group. It is the home for one semester each year of Nobel laureate poet Seamus Heaney.

Right: Russet-topped Dunster House (1930) clock tower, modeled on Big Tom Tower of Christchurch, Oxford.

The heart of commercial Cambridge, Harvard Square is no square at all, but instead a traffic island where Massachusetts Avenue widens into a big triangle. The copper-topped, Art Deco kiosk (1928) houses Out of Town News, a local landmark. The domed information booth sits beside the Harvard "T" station. The sculpture on the near end of the island is Omphalos, Greek for "navel," signifying in many Cantabrigian's minds the square's position as center of the universe. Cambridge has abundant bookstores that line the streets and is second only to Wales in Great Britain for the greatest number of bookstores per capita.

The 35-acre campus on the south side of the Charles River is the Harvard Business School. Founded in 1908, the HBS was initially conceived as a "delicate experiment" in the new field of professional management training, and was the first university to require a college degree for admission to its business program.

Also on the south side of the Charles, opposite Cambridge and the river houses (*inset*), Harvard Stadium at Soldier's Field was designed by George Bruno de Gernsdorff after an Athenian model and constructed in 1903.

When Roxbury was incorporated into Boston in 1868, it was a quiet, middle-class streetcar suburb. During the twentieth century, Roxbury became a port of entry for various ethnic groups, and today it is one of the city's historic African American districts. *Above*: Fort Hill once stood much higher, but it was lowered after the Civil War to provide landfill along Boston's waterfront. Atop the hill, a nineteenth-century Gothic water tower with observation balcony.

Right: View of south Tremont Street, with Mission Church. In 1869, Boston's archbishop invited the Redemptorists to Boston; they founded Our Lady of Perpetual Help and constructed this granite edifice in 1878. The soaring Gothic, twin towers were completed in 1910. Pope Pius XII declared the church a basilica in 1954.

INDEX

ACKNOWLEDGMENTS

The publisher wishes to thank Simon Clay for taking all the photography for this book, including the photographs on the front and back covers.